Intellectual Property Act 2014

CHAPTER 18

Explanatory Notes are available separately

GRANG*IS* UK Publishing

Adapted and published by GRANGIS (Grand Register Library).
Online: www.grangis.com
E-mail: contact@grangis.com

In this version:
ISBN: 979-8-88559-055-6

Note: This is the original version (as it was originally enacted). Title, sub-title and the generated date is as marked on the pages.

Intellectual Property Act 2014

CHAPTER 18

INTELLECTUAL PROPERTY ACT 2014

PART 1

DESIGN

Unregistered design right

Registered Community design

Registered designs

PART 2

PATENTS

PART 3

MISCELLANEOUS

PART 4

GENERAL

Intellectual Property Act 2014

2014 CHAPTER 18

An Act to make provision about intellectual property. [14th May 2014]

BE IT ENACTED by the Queen's most Excellent Majesty, by and with the advice and consent of the Lords Spiritual and Temporal, and Commons, in this present Parliament assembled, and by the authority of the same, as follows:—

PART 1

DESIGN

Unregistered design right

1 Meaning of "design" and "original"

(1) In section 213(2) of the Copyright, Designs and Patents Act 1988 (unregistered design right: meaning of "design"), in subsection (2), omit "any aspect of".

(2) In section 51 of that Act (copyright infringement: exception for certain designs), in subsection (3), in the definition of "design", omit "any aspect of".

(3) In section 213(4) of that Act (unregistered design right: meaning of "original")—

(a) after "commonplace" insert "in a qualifying country", and

(b) at the end insert "; and "qualifying country" has the meaning given in section 217(3)".

(4) Subsection (3) applies only to designs created after the commencement of that subsection.

2 Ownership of design

(1) In section 215 of the Copyright, Designs and Patents Act 1988 (ownership of unregistered design right)—

(a) in subsection (1), omit "in pursuance of a commission or",

(b) omit subsection (2), and

(c) in subsection (3), omit ", in a case not falling within subsection (2)".

(2) In consequence of subsection (1)—

(a) in section 213(5)(a) of that Act (person by reference to whom design qualifies for design right), for "the design was commissioned or the designer employed" substitute "the designer was employed",

(b) in section 218 of that Act (design qualifies for design right by reference to designer), in subsection (1), omit "in pursuance of a commission or",

(c) in section 219 of that Act (the title to which becomes "Qualification by reference to employer"), in subsection (1), for "in pursuance of a commission from, or in the course of employment with," substitute "in the course of employment with",

(d) in subsection (2) of that section, omit "a joint commission or" and "commissioners or",

(e) in subsection (3) of that section, omit "jointly commissioned or", "commissioners or" and "commissioner or",

(f) in that subsection, for "215(2) or (3)" substitute "215(3)",

(g) in section 220 of that Act (qualification by reference to first marketing), in subsection (1), omit ", commissioner",

(h) in subsection (4)(a) of that section, omit ", commissioner of the design",

(i) in section 263 of that Act (definitions), in subsection (1), in the definition of "British design", omit "the design is commissioned or",

(j) in that subsection, omit the definition of "commission", and

(k) in section 264 of that Act (index of defined expressions), omit the entry for "commission".

(3) This section does not apply to—

(a) any design created before the commencement of this section, or

(b) any design created after the commencement of this section in pursuance of a commission (irrespective of whether the design was commissioned before or after that commencement) provided that—

(i) the designer and the commissioner of the design have entered into a contract relating to the commission of the design, and

(ii) the contract was entered into before that commencement.

3 Qualification criteria

(1) In section 217 of that Act (qualifying individuals and qualifying persons), in subsection (1)—

(a) omit the definition of "qualifying individual", and

(b) for the definition of "qualifying person" substitute—

""qualifying person" means—

(a) an individual habitually resident in a qualifying country, or

(b) a body corporate or other body having legal personality which—

(i) is formed under the law of a part of the United Kingdom or another qualifying country, and

(ii) has in any qualifying country a place of business at which substantial business activity is carried on."

(2) In that section, omit subsection (4).

(3) In section 218 of that Act (qualification by reference to designer)—

(a) in subsection (2), omit "a qualifying individual or, in the case of a computer-generated design,"

(b) in subsection (3), omit "a qualifying individual or, as the case may be,", and

(c) in subsection (4), omit "qualifying individuals or".

(4) In section 220 of that Act (qualification by reference to first marketing)—

(a) in subsection (1)(a), omit "who is exclusively authorised to put such articles on the market in the United Kingdom",

(b) in subsection (2), for "requirements" substitute "requirement",

(c) in subsection (3), for "those requirements" substitute "that requirement", and

(d) omit subsection (4).

(5) In section 264 of that Act (index of defined expressions), in the Table, omit the entry for "qualifying individual".

(6) This section applies only to designs created after the commencement of this section.

4 Infringement: exceptions

After section 244 of the Copyright, Designs and Patents Act 1988 (but before the following cross-heading) insert—

"Miscellaneous

244A Exception for private acts, experiments and teaching

Design right is not infringed by—

(a) an act which is done privately and for purposes which are not commercial;

(b) an act which is done for experimental purposes; or

(c) an act of reproduction for teaching purposes or for the purpose of making citations provided that—

(i) the act of reproduction is compatible with fair trade practice and does not unduly prejudice the normal exploitation of the design, and

(ii) mention is made of the source.

244B Exception for overseas ships and aircraft

Design right is not infringed by—

(a) the use of equipment on ships or aircraft which are registered in another country but which are temporarily in the United Kingdom;

(b) the importation into the United Kingdom of spare parts or accessories for the purpose of repairing such ships or aircraft; or

(c) the carrying out of repairs on such ships or aircraft."

Registered Community design

5 Infringement: exception

(1) Section 53 of the Copyright, Designs and Patents Act 1988 (permitted acts in relation to copyright works: things done in reliance on registration of design) is amended as follows.

(2) In subsection (1), in paragraph (a)—

(a) after "registered" insert "—

(i)",

and

(b) after "corresponding design" insert ", or

(ii) under the Community Design Regulation as the right holder of a corresponding registered Community design".

(3) In paragraph (b) of that subsection, after "the registration or" insert ", in a case of registration under the 1949 Act,".

(4) At the end of that subsection, insert "or, in a case of registration under the Community Design Regulation, that the person registered as the right holder was not the right holder of the design for the purposes of the Regulation".

(5) After subsection (2), insert—

"(3) In subsection (1), a "corresponding registered Community design", in relation to an artistic work, means a design within the meaning of the Community Design Regulation which if applied to an article would produce something which would be treated for the purposes of this Part as a copy of the artistic work."

(6) After subsection (3), insert—

"(4) In this section, "the Community Design Regulation" means Council Regulation (EC) No 6/2002 of 12 December 2001 on Community designs."

Registered designs

6 Ownership of design and application for registration

(1) In section 2 of the Registered Designs Act 1949 (ownership of registered designs)—

(a) omit subsection (1A) (which provides for the commissioner of a design to be the original proprietor), and

(b) in subsection (1B), omit ", in a case not falling within subsection (1A),".

(2) In section 3 of that Act (application for registration), omit subsection (2) (requirement for application to be made by person claiming to be proprietor).

7 Right of prior use

(1) After section 7A of the Registered Designs Act 1949 insert—

"7B Right of prior use

(1) A person who, before the application date, used a registered design in good faith or made serious and effective preparations to do so may continue to use the design for the purposes for which, before that date, the person had used it or made the preparations to use it.

(2) In subsection (1), the "application date", in relation to a registered design, means—

(a) the date on which an application for the registration was made under section 3, or

(b) where an application for the registration was treated as having been made by virtue of section 14(2), the date on which it was treated as having been so made.

(3) Subsection (1) does not apply if the design which the person used, or made preparations to use, was copied from the design which was subsequently registered.

(4) The right conferred on a person by subsection (1) does not include a right to licence another person to use the design.

(5) Nor may the person on whom the right under subsection (1) is conferred assign the right, or transmit it on death (or in the case of a body corporate on its dissolution), unless—

(a) the design was used, or the preparations for its use were made, in the course of a business, and

(b) the right is assigned or transmitted with the part of the business in which the design was used or the preparations for its use were made."

(2) This section applies only to designs registered under the Registered Designs Act 1949 after the commencement of this section.

8 Accession to the Hague Agreement

(1) After section 15 of the Registered Designs Act 1949 insert—

"15ZA Accession to the Hague Agreement

(1) The Secretary of State may by order make provision for giving effect in the United Kingdom to the provisions of the Geneva Act of the Hague Agreement Concerning the International Registration of Industrial Designs adopted by the Diplomatic Conference on 2 July 1999.

(2) An order under this section may, in particular, make provision about—

(a) the making of applications for international registrations at the Patent Office;

(b) the procedures to be followed where an international registration designates the United Kingdom;

(c) the effect of an international registration which designates the United Kingdom;

(d) the communication of information to the International Bureau;

(e) the payment of fees.

(3) An order under this section may—

(a) amend this Act;

(b) apply specified provisions of this Act with such modifications as may be specified.

(4) An expression used in subsection (2) and in the Agreement referred to in subsection (1) has the same meaning in that subsection as it has in the Agreement."

(2) In section 37 of that Act (rules and orders)—

(a) in subsection (3), before "shall be exercisable" insert "and the power to make an order under section 15ZA", and

(b) before subsection (5) insert—

"(4B) The Secretary of State may not make an order under section 15ZA unless a draft of the statutory instrument containing the order has been laid before, and approved by a resolution of, each House of Parliament."

9 The register: changes of ownership and inspection of documents

(1) In section 19 of the Registered Designs Act 1949 (registration of assignments, etc.), omit subsection (3A) (which, where design right subsists in a registered design, prohibits the registrar from registering an interest unless satisfied that the person who has the interest has a corresponding interest in the design right).

(2) In section 22 of that Act (the title to which becomes "Inspection of registered designs and associated documents"), in subsection (1), after paragraph (a) insert "and

(aa) every document kept at the Patent Office in connection with that design."

(3) In that subsection, for "subsection (4)" substitute "subsections (4) to (7)".

(4) After subsection (4) of that section insert—

"(5) For the purposes of subsection (1), a document is not to be regarded as open for inspection unless (in addition to being open for inspection in hard copy) it is made available by electronic transmission in such a way that members of the public may access it at a place and time individually chosen by them."

(5) After subsection (5) insert—

"(6) The Secretary of State may by rules specify cases or circumstances in which a document kept at the Patent Office in connection with a registered design may not be inspected.

(7) Rules made under subsection (6) may confer a discretion on the registrar."

(6) In section 37 of that Act (rules and orders), in subsection (2), after "section 15" insert "or 22(6)".

10 Legal proceedings and appeals

(1) In section 24B of the Registered Designs Act 1949 (exemption of innocent infringer from liability), in subsection (1), omit ", and no order shall be made for an account of profits,".

(2) After section 27 of that Act insert—

"27A Appeals from decisions of registrar

(1) An appeal against a decision of the registrar under this Act may be made to—
- (a) a person appointed by the Lord Chancellor (an "appointed person"), or
- (b) the court.

(2) On an appeal under this section to an appointed person, the appointed person may refer the appeal to the court if—
- (a) it appears to the appointed person that a point of general legal importance is involved,
- (b) the registrar requests that the appeal be so referred, or
- (c) such a request is made by any party to the proceedings before the registrar in which the decision appealed against was made.

(3) Before referring an appeal to the court under subsection (2), the appointed person must give the appellant and any other party to the appeal an opportunity to make representations as to whether it should be so referred.

(4) Where, on an appeal under this section to an appointed person, the appointed person does not refer the appeal to the court—
- (a) the appointed person must hear and determine the appeal, and
- (b) the appointed person's decision is final.

(5) Sections 30 and 31 (costs, evidence) apply to proceedings before an appointed person as they apply to proceedings before the registrar.

(6) In the application of this section to England and Wales, "the court" means the High Court.

27B Persons appointed to hear and determine appeals

(1) A person is not eligible for appointment under section 27A(1)(a) unless the person—
- (a) satisfies the judicial-appointment eligibility condition on a 5-year basis,
- (b) is an advocate or solicitor in Scotland of at least 5 years' standing,
- (c) is a member of the Bar of Northern Ireland or solicitor of the Court of Judicature of Northern Ireland of at least 5 years' standing, or
- (d) has held judicial office.

(2) An appointed person must hold and vacate office in accordance with his terms of appointment, subject to subsections (3) to (5).

(3) An appointed person is to be paid such remuneration (whether by way of salary or fees) and such allowances as the Secretary of State may with the approval of the Treasury decide.

(4) An appointed person may resign office by notice in writing to the Lord Chancellor.

(5) The Lord Chancellor may by notice in writing remove an appointed person ("A") from office if—

(a) A has become bankrupt or made an arrangement with A's creditors or, in Scotland, A's estate has been sequestrated or A has executed a trust deed for A's creditors or entered into a composition contract,

(b) A is incapacitated by physical or mental illness, or

(c) A is, in the opinion of the Lord Chancellor, otherwise unable or unfit to perform A's duties as an appointed person.

(6) Before exercising a power under section 27A or this section, the Lord Chancellor must consult the Secretary of State.

(7) The Lord Chancellor may remove a person from office under subsection (5) only with the concurrence of the appropriate senior judge.

(8) The appropriate senior judge is the Lord Chief Justice of England and Wales, unless—

(a) the person to be removed exercises functions wholly or mainly in Scotland, in which case it is the Lord President of the Court of Session, or

(b) the person to be removed exercises functions wholly or mainly in Northern Ireland, in which case it is the Lord Chief Justice of Northern Ireland."

(3) In section 27(1)(a) of that Act, after "the High Court or" insert "(subject to section 27A(6))".

(4) Section 28 of that Act (the Appeal Tribunal) is repealed.

(5) In section 37(3) of that Act (provision as to rules and orders)—

(a) omit "or on the Appeal Tribunal", and

(b) omit the words from "; and the Statutory Instruments Act 1946" to the end.

(6) In section 44(1) of that Act (interpretation), omit the definition of "Appeal Tribunal".

(7) In section 249 of the Copyright, Designs and Patents Act 1988 (right of appeal as to terms of licence of right)—

(a) in subsection (1), for the words from "the Appeal Tribunal" to the end substitute "a person appointed under section 27A of the Registered Designs Act 1949", and

(b) omit subsection (2).

(8) In section 251(4) of that Act (right of appeal against decisions of comptroller relating to design right)—

(a) before "the High Court" insert "—

(a)",

and

(b) at the end insert ", or

(b) a person appointed under section 27A of the Registered Designs Act 1949".

(9) In the House of Commons Disqualification Act 1975, in Schedule 1 (offices disqualifying for membership), in Part 3 (other disqualifying offices), at the appropriate place insert—

"Person appointed under section 27A of the Registered Designs Act 1949 to hear and determine appeals against decisions of the registrar under that Act".

(10) In the Constitutional Reform Act 2005, in Schedule 7 (protected functions of the Lord Chancellor), in paragraph 4, at the appropriate place insert—

"Registered Designs Act 1949 (c.88)

Sections 27A and 27B."

(11) Section 143 of the Tribunals, Courts and Enforcement Act 2007 (which makes provision about appeals in relation to design rights) is repealed.

11 Opinions service

(1) Before section 29 of the Registered Designs Act 1949 (and the preceding cross-heading) insert—

"Opinions service

28A Opinions on designs

(1) The Secretary of State may by regulations make provision about the making of requests to the registrar for an opinion on specified matters relating to—

(a) designs registered under this Act;

(b) designs of such other description as may be specified.

(2) The regulations must require the registrar to give an opinion in response to a request made under the regulations, except—

(a) in specified cases or circumstances, or

(b) where for any reason the registrar considers it inappropriate in all the circumstances to do so.

(3) The regulations may provide that a request made under the regulations must be accompanied by—

(a) a fee of a specified amount;

(b) specified information.

(4) The regulations must provide that an opinion given by the registrar under the regulations is not binding for any purposes.

(5) The regulations must provide that neither the registrar nor any examiner or other officer of the Patent Office is to incur any liability by reason of or in connection with—

(a) any opinion given under the regulations, or

(b) any examination or investigation undertaken for the purpose of giving such an opinion.

(6) An opinion given by the registrar under the regulations is not to be treated as a decision of the registrar for the purposes of section 27A.

(7) But the regulations must provide for an appeal relating to an opinion given under the regulations to be made to a person appointed under section 27A; and the regulations may make further provision in relation to such appeals.

(8) The regulations may confer discretion on the registrar.

(9) Regulations under this section—

(a) may make different provision for different purposes;

(b) may include consequential, incidental, supplementary, transitional, transitory or saving provision.

(10) In this section, "specified" means specified in regulations under this section."

(2) In Chapter 4 of Part 3 of the Copyright, Designs and Patents Act 1988 (jurisdiction of the comptroller etc.), after section 249 insert—

"249A Opinions service

The descriptions of designs which may be specified in regulations under subsection (1)(b) of section 28A of the Registered Designs Act 1949 (requests to the comptroller for opinions on designs) include, in particular—

(a) designs in which design right subsists in accordance with this Part, and

(b) designs in relation to which there is a question whether design right so subsists."

(3) In section 37 of the Registered Designs Act 1949 (the title to which becomes "Provisions as to rules, regulations and orders")—

(a) in subsection (3), after "an order under section 15ZA" (inserted by section 8(2)(a)), insert "and the power to make regulations under section 28A",

(b) in subsection (4), after "under this Act" insert "or regulations under section 28A", and

(c) after subsection (4) insert—

"(4A) Subsection (4) does not apply to the first regulations to be made under section 28A, but the Secretary of State may not make those regulations unless a draft of the statutory instrument containing them has been laid before, and approved by a resolution of, each House of Parliament."

12 Use of directions by the registrar

(1) After section 31 of the Registered Designs Act 1949 insert—

"31A Power to require use of forms

(1) The registrar may require the use of such forms as the registrar may direct for—

(a) an application for the registration of a design;

(b) representations or specimens of designs or other documents which may be filed at the Patent Office.

(2) The forms, and any directions by the registrar about their use, are to be published in the prescribed manner."

(2) In section 3(1) of that Act (application for registration), omit "shall be made in the prescribed form and".

(3) In section 36(1A) of that Act (matters which may be covered in rules), for paragraph (a) substitute—

"(a) requiring the furnishing of copies of such representations or specimens of designs or other documents as may be filed at the Patent Office;".

(4) In section 39(1) of that Act (hours of business and excluded days)—

(a) for "Rules made by the Secretary of State under this Act may specify" substitute "The registrar may give directions specifying", and

(b) for "and may specify" substitute "and specifying".

(5) Despite the repeal made by subsection (2), any rules made in reliance on section 3(1) of that Act which are in force immediately before the commencement of that repeal continue in force until such time as directions about forms of the kind which had been prescribed by the rules take effect.

(6) Despite the amendment made by subsection (3), any rules made in reliance on section 36(1A)(a) of that Act which are in force immediately before the commencement of that amendment continue in force until such time as directions about forms of the kind which had been prescribed by the rules take effect.

(7) In subsections (5) and (6), "directions" means directions given under section 31A of that Act (as inserted by subsection (1)).

(8) Despite the amendment made by subsection (4), any rules made in reliance on section 39(1) of that Act which are in force immediately before the commencement of that amendment continue in force until such time as directions about the matter specified by the rules take effect.

(9) In subsection (8), "directions" means directions given under section 39(1) of that Act (as amended by subsection (4)).

13 Offence of unauthorised copying etc. of design in course of business

After section 35 of the Registered Designs Act 1949 insert—

"35ZA Offence of unauthorised copying etc. of design in course of business

(1) A person commits an offence if—

(a) in the course of a business, the person intentionally copies a registered design so as to make a product—

(i) exactly to that design, or

(ii) with features that differ only in immaterial details from that design, and

(b) the person does so—
(i) knowing, or having reason to believe, that the design is a registered design, and
(ii) without the consent of the registered proprietor of the design.

(2) Subsection (3) applies in relation to a product where a registered design has been intentionally copied so as to make the product—
(a) exactly to the design, or
(b) with features that differ only in immaterial details from the design.

(3) A person commits an offence if—
(a) in the course of a business, the person offers, puts on the market, imports, exports or uses the product, or stocks it for one or more of those purposes,
(b) the person does so without the consent of the registered proprietor of the design, and
(c) the person does so knowing, or having reason to believe, that—
(i) a design has been intentionally copied without the consent of the registered proprietor so as to make the product exactly to the design or with features that differ only in immaterial details from the design, and
(ii) the design is a registered design.

(4) It is a defence for a person charged with an offence under this section to show that the person reasonably believed that the registration of the design was invalid.

(5) It is also a defence for a person charged with an offence under this section to show that the person—
(a) did not infringe the right in the design, or
(b) reasonably believed that the person did not do so.

(6) The reference in subsection (3) to using a product in the course of a business does not include a reference to using it for a purpose which is merely incidental to the carrying on of the business.

(7) In this section "registered design" includes a registered Community design; and a reference to the registered proprietor is, in the case of a registered Community design, to be read as a reference to the holder.

(8) A person guilty of an offence under this section is liable—
(a) on conviction on indictment, to imprisonment for a term not exceeding ten years or to a fine or to both;
(b) on summary conviction in England and Wales or Northern Ireland, to imprisonment for a term not exceeding six months or to a fine not exceeding the statutory maximum or to both;
(c) on summary conviction in Scotland, to imprisonment for a term not exceeding 12 months or to a fine not exceeding the statutory maximum or to both.

35ZB Section 35ZA: enforcement

(1) The following provisions of the Trade Descriptions Act 1968 (which provide for the enforcement of that Act by local weights and measures authorities or the relevant Northern Ireland Department) apply as if section 35ZA were a provision of that Act—

(a) section 27 (power to make test purchases);

(b) section 28 (power to enter premises and inspect and seize goods and documents);

(c) section 29 (obstruction of authorised officers);

(d) section 33 (compensation for loss etc. of seized goods).

(2) Any enactment which authorises the disclosure of information for the purpose of facilitating the enforcement of the Trade Descriptions Act 1968 applies—

(a) as if section 35ZA were a provision of that Act, and

(b) as if the functions of any person in relation to the enforcement of that section were functions under that Act.

(3) Nothing in this section is to be construed as authorising a local weights and measures authority to bring proceedings in Scotland.

35ZC Section 35ZA: forfeiture in England and Wales or Northern Ireland

(1) In England and Wales or Northern Ireland, a person who, in connection with the investigation or prosecution of an offence under section 35ZA, has come into the possession of relevant products or articles may apply under this section for an order for the forfeiture of the products or articles.

(2) "Relevant product" means a product which is made exactly to a registered design, or with features that differ only in immaterial details from a registered design, by copying that design intentionally.

(3) "Relevant article" means an article which is specifically designed or adapted for making copies of a registered design intentionally.

(4) An application under this section may be made—

(a) where proceedings have been brought in any court for an offence under section 35ZA relating to some or all of the products or articles, to that court;

(b) where no application for the forfeiture of the products or articles has been made under paragraph (a), by way of complaint to a magistrates' court.

(5) On an application under this section, the court may make an order for the forfeiture of products or articles only if it is satisfied that an offence under section 35ZA has been committed in relation to the products or articles.

(6) A court may infer for the purposes of this section that such an offence has been committed in relation to any products or articles if it is satisfied that such an offence has been committed in relation to products or articles which are representations of them (whether by reason of being of the same design or part of the same consignment or batch or otherwise).

(7) Any person aggrieved by an order made under this section by a magistrates' court, or by a decision of such a court not to make such an order, may appeal against that order or decision—

(a) in England and Wales, to the Crown Court;

(b) in Northern Ireland, to the county court.

(8) An order so made may contain such provision as appears to the court to be appropriate for delaying the coming into force of the order pending the making and determination of any appeal (including any application under section 111 of the Magistrates' Courts Act 1980 or Article 146 of the Magistrates' Courts (Northern Ireland) Order 1981).

(9) Subject to subsection (10), any products or articles forfeited under this section are to be destroyed in accordance with such directions as the court may give.

(10) On making an order under this section, the court may, if it considers it appropriate to do so, direct that the products or articles to which the order relates shall (instead of being destroyed) be released to such person and on such conditions as the court may specify.

35ZD Section 35ZA: forfeiture in Scotland

(1) In Scotland, the court may make an order for the forfeiture of any relevant products or articles (as defined by section 35ZC).

(2) An order under this section may be made—

(a) on an application by the procurator fiscal made in the manner specified in section 134 of the Criminal Procedure (Scotland) Act 1995, or

(b) where a person is convicted of an offence under section 35ZA, in addition to any other penalty which the court may impose.

(3) On an application under subsection (2)(a), the court may make an order for the forfeiture of relevant products or articles only if it is satisfied that an offence under section 35ZA has been committed in relation to the relevant products or articles.

(4) The court may infer for the purposes of this section that such an offence has been committed in relation to any relevant products or articles which are representative of them (whether by reason of being of the same design or part of the same consignment or batch or otherwise).

(5) The procurator fiscal making the application under subsection (2)(a) must serve on any person appearing to the procurator fiscal to be the owner of, or otherwise have an interest in, the products or articles to which an application under this section relates is entitled to appear at the hearing of the application to show cause why the products or articles should not be forfeited.

(6) Service under subsection (5) must be carried out, and such service may be proved, in the manner specified for citation of an accused in summary proceedings under the Criminal Procedure (Scotland) Act 1995.

(7) Any person upon whom notice is served under subsection (5) and any other person claiming to be the owner of, or otherwise have an interest in, products or articles to which an application under this section relates is entitled to appear at

the hearing of the application to show cause why the products or articles should not be forfeited.

(8) The court must not make an order following an application under subsection (2)(a)—

(a) if any person on whom notice is served under subsection (5) does not appear, unless service of the notice on that person is proved, or

(b) if no notice under subsection (5) has been served, unless the court is satisfied that in the circumstances it was reasonable not to serve such notice.

(9) Where an order for the forfeiture of any products or articles is made following an application under subsection (2)(a), any person who appeared, or was entitled to appear, to show cause why goods, material or articles should not be forfeited may, within 21 days of making the order, appeal to the High Court of Justiciary by bill of suspension.

(10) Section 182(5)(a) to (e) of the Criminal Procedure (Scotland) Act 1995 applies to an appeal under subsection (9) as it applies to a stated case under Part 2 of that Act.

(11) An order following an application under subsection (2)(a) does not take effect—

(a) until the end of the period of 21 days beginning with the day after the day on which the order is made, or

(b) if an appeal is made under subsection (9) within that period, until the appeal is dismissed or abandoned.

(12) An order under subsection (2)(b) does not take effect—

(a) until the end of the period within which an appeal against the order could be brought under the Criminal Procedure (Scotland) Act 1995, or

(b) if an appeal is made within that period, until the appeal is determined or abandoned.

(13) Subject to subsection (14), products or articles forfeited under this section must be destroyed in accordance with such directions as the court may give.

(14) On making an order under this section, the court may, if it considers it appropriate to do so, direct that the products or articles to which the order relates shall (instead of being destroyed) be released, to such person and on such conditions as the court may specify.

(15) In this section, "the court" means—

(a) in relation to an order made on an application under subsection (2)(a), the sheriff;

(b) in relation to an order made under subsection (2)(b), the court which imposed the penalty."

14 Offences committed by partnerships

At the end of section 35A of the Registered Designs Act 1949 (the title to which becomes "Offence by body corporate or partnership: liability of officers or partners") insert—

"(3) Proceedings for an offence under this Act alleged to have been committed by a partnership are to be brought against the partnership in the name of the firm and not in that of the partners; but without prejudice to any liability of the partners under subsection (6) or (7).

(4) The following provisions apply for the purposes of such proceedings as in relation to a body corporate—

(a) any rules of court relating to the service of documents;

(b) in England and Wales, Schedule 3 to the Magistrates' Courts Act 1980;

(c) in Northern Ireland, Schedule 4 to the Magistrates' Courts (Northern Ireland) Order 1981.

(5) A fine imposed on a partnership (other than a Scottish partnership) on its conviction in such proceedings must be paid out of the partnership assets.

(6) Where a partnership (other than a Scottish partnership) is guilty of an offence under this Act, every partner, other than a partner who is proved to have been ignorant of or to have attempted to prevent the commission of the offence, is also guilty of the offence and liable to be proceeded against and punished accordingly.

(7) Where an offence under this Act committed by a Scottish partnership is proved to have been committed with the consent or connivance of a partner in the partnership, or a person purporting to act in that capacity, he as well as the partnership is guilty of the offence and liable to be proceeded against and punished accordingly."

PART 2

PATENTS

15 Infringement: marking product with internet link

(1) In section 62 of the Patents Act 1977 (restrictions on recovery of damages for infringement), in subsection (1), after "the number of the patent" insert "or a relevant internet link".

(2) After that subsection insert—

"(1A) The reference in subsection (1) to a relevant internet link is a reference to an address of a posting on the internet—

(a) which is accessible to the public free of charge, and

(b) which clearly associates the product with the number of the patent."

16 Opinions service

(1) In section 74A of the Patents Act 1977 (the title to which becomes "Opinions on matters prescribed in the rules"), in subsection (1), for the words from "an opinion" to the end substitute "an opinion on a prescribed matter in relation to the patent".

(2) In section 74B of that Act (reviews of opinions under section 74A), omit subsection (2)(c) (power to make rules providing for review proceedings to be treated as other proceedings under the Act).

(3) In Schedule 4A to that Act (application of Act to supplementary protection certificates), in paragraph 1(2), at the appropriate place insert—

"sections 74A and 74B (opinions by the Patent Office);".

(4) In section 73 of that Act (comptroller's power to revoke patents), after subsection (1) insert—

"(1A) Where the comptroller issues an opinion under section 74A that section 1(1)(a) or (b) is not satisfied in relation to an invention for which there is a patent, the comptroller may revoke the patent.

(1B) The power under subsection (1A) may not be exercised before—

(a) the end of the period in which the proprietor of the patent may apply under the rules (by virtue of section 74B) for a review of the opinion, or

(b) if the proprietor applies for a review, the decision on the review is made (or, if there is an appeal against that decision, the appeal is determined).

(1C) The comptroller shall not exercise the power under subsection (1A) without giving the proprietor of the patent an opportunity to make any observations and to amend the specification of the patent without contravening section 76."

17 Unified Patent Court

Before section 89 of the Patents Act 1977 (and before the preceding cross-heading) insert—

"Unified Patent Court

88A Implementation of Agreement on a Unified Patent Court

(1) The Secretary of State may by order make provision for giving effect in the United Kingdom to the provisions of the Agreement on a Unified Patent Court made in Brussels on 19 February 2013.

(2) An order under this section may, in particular, make provision—

(a) to confer jurisdiction on a court, remove jurisdiction from a court or vary the jurisdiction of a court;

(b) to require the payment of fees.

(3) An order under this section may also make provision for varying the application of specified provisions of this Act so that they correspond to provision made by the Agreement.

(4) An order under this section may—

(a) make provision which applies generally or in relation only to specified cases;

(b) make different provision for different cases.

(5) An order under this section may amend this Act or any other enactment.

(6) An order under this section may not be made unless a draft of the order has been laid before, and approved by resolution of, each House of Parliament.

(7) The meaning of "court" in this section is not limited by the definition of that expression in section 130(1).

88B Designation as international organisation of which UK is member

The Unified Patent Court is to be treated for the purposes of section 1 of the International Organisations Act 1968 (organisations of which the United Kingdom is a member) as an organisation to which that section applies."

18 Sharing information with overseas patent offices

(1) In section 118 of the Patents Act 1977 (information on patent applications etc.), in subsection (3), after paragraph (a) (but before the following "or") insert—

"(aa) sending any patent office outside the United Kingdom such information about unpublished applications for patents as that office requests;".

(2) After that subsection insert—

"(3A) Information may not be sent to a patent office in reliance on subsection (3)(aa) otherwise than in accordance with the working arrangements that the comptroller has made for that purpose with that office.

(3B) Those arrangements must include provision for ensuring that the confidentiality of information of the kind referred to in subsection (3)(aa) sent by the comptroller to the patent office in question is protected."

(3) After subsection (3B) insert—

"(3C) The reference in subsection (3)(aa) to a patent office is to an organisation which carries out, in relation to patents, functions of the kind carried out at the Patent Office."

19 Minor amendments to the Patents Act 1977

The Schedule (which makes minor amendments to the Patents Act 1977) has effect.

PART 3

MISCELLANEOUS

20 Freedom of information: exemption for research

After section 22 of the Freedom of Information Act 2000, insert—

"22A Research

(1) Information obtained in the course of, or derived from, a programme of research is exempt information if—

(a) the programme is continuing with a view to the publication, by a public authority or any other person, of a report of the research (whether or not including a statement of that information), and

(b) disclosure of the information under this Act before the date of publication would, or would be likely to, prejudice—

(i) the programme,

(ii) the interests of any individual participating in the programme,

(iii) the interests of the authority which holds the information, or

(iv) the interests of the authority mentioned in paragraph (a) (if it is a different authority from that which holds the information).

(2) The duty to confirm or deny does not arise in relation to information which is (or if it were held by the public authority would be) exempt information by virtue of subsection (1) if, or to the extent that, compliance with section 1(1)(a) would, or would be likely to, prejudice any of the matters mentioned in subsection (1)(b)."

21 Reporting duty

(1) The Secretary of State must, before the end of the period of 6 months beginning with the end of each financial year, lay before Parliament a report setting out—

(a) the Secretary of State's opinion of the extent to which during that year—

(i) the activities of the Patent Office have contributed to the promotion of innovation and of economic growth in the United Kingdom, and

(ii) legislation relating to intellectual property has been effective in facilitating innovation and economic growth in the United Kingdom, and

(b) how the promotion of innovation and of economic growth in the United Kingdom was taken into account in the case of any legislation relating to intellectual property that was passed or made during that year.

(2) The reference to the activities of the Patent Office is a reference to—

(a) the activities of the comptroller-general of patents, designs and trade marks, and

(b) the activities of the officers and clerks of the Patent Office.

(3) The references to legislation relating to intellectual property do not include a reference to legislation relating to plant breeders' rights or rights under section 7 of the Plant Varieties Act 1997.

(4) "Financial year" means a period of 12 months ending with 31 March.

(5) "Legislation" includes—

(a) subordinate legislation within the meaning of the Interpretation Act 1978, and

(b) legislation of the European Union.

22 Recognition of foreign copyright works and performances

(1) In section 154 of the Copyright, Designs and Patents Act 1988 (qualification by reference to author), in subsection (1)—

(a) in paragraph (a), after "a British citizen," insert "a national of another EEA state,",

(b) for paragraph (b) (but not the following "or") substitute—

"(b) an individual domiciled or resident in the United Kingdom or another EEA state or in the Channel Islands, the Isle of Man or Gibraltar or in a country to which the relevant provisions of this Part extend,", and

(c) for paragraph (c) substitute—

"(c) a body incorporated under the law of a part of the United Kingdom or another EEA state or of the Channel Islands, the Isle of Man or Gibraltar or of a country to which the relevant provisions of this Part extend."

(2) In section 155 of that Act (qualification by reference to country of first publication), in subsection (1)—

(a) in paragraph (a), after "the United Kingdom" insert ", another EEA state, the Channel Islands, the Isle of Man or Gibraltar", and

(b) in paragraph (b), for "another country" substitute "a country".

(3) In section 156 of that Act (qualification by reference to place of transmission), in subsection (1)—

(a) in paragraph (a), after "the United Kingdom" insert ", another EEA state, the Channel Islands, the Isle of Man or Gibraltar", and

(b) in paragraph (b), for "another country" substitute "a country".

(4) For section 159 of that Act substitute—

"159 Application of this Part to countries to which it does not extend

(1) Where a country is a party to the Berne Convention or a member of the World Trade Organisation, this Part, so far as it relates to literary, dramatic, musical and artistic works, films and typographical arrangements of published editions—

(a) applies in relation to a citizen or subject of that country or a person domiciled or resident there as it applies in relation to a person who is a British citizen or is domiciled or resident in the United Kingdom,

(b) applies in relation to a body incorporated under the law of that country as it applies in relation to a body incorporated under the law of a part of the United Kingdom, and

(c) applies in relation to a work first published in that country as it applies in relation to a work first published in the United Kingdom.

(2) Where a country is a party to the Rome Convention, this Part, so far as it relates to sound recordings and broadcasts—

(a) applies in relation to that country as mentioned in paragraphs (a), (b) and (c) of subsection (1), and

(b) applies in relation to a broadcast made from that country as it applies to a broadcast made from the United Kingdom.

(3) Where a country is a party to the WPPT, this Part, so far as relating to sound recordings, applies in relation to that country as mentioned in paragraphs (a), (b) and (c) of subsection (1).

(4) Her Majesty may by Order in Council—

(a) make provision for the application of this Part to a country by subsection (1), (2) or (3) to be subject to specified restrictions;

(b) make provision for applying this Part, or any of its provisions, to a specified country;

(c) make provision for applying this Part, or any of its provisions, to any country of a specified description;

(d) make provision for the application of legislation to a country under paragraph (b) or (c) to be subject to specified restrictions.

(5) Provision made under subsection (4) may apply generally or in relation to such classes of works, or other classes of case, as are specified.

(6) Her Majesty may not make an Order in Council containing provision under subsection (4)(b) or (c) unless satisfied that provision has been or will be made under the law of the country or countries in question, in respect of the classes to which the provision under subsection (4)(b) or (c) relates, giving adequate protection to the owners of copyright under this Part.

(7) Application under subsection (4)(b) or (c) is in addition to application by subsections (1) to (3).

(8) Provision made under subsection (4)(c) may cover countries that become (or again become) of the specified description after the provision comes into force.

(9) In this section—

"the Berne Convention" means any Act of the International Convention for the Protection of Literary and Artistic Works signed at Berne on 9 September 1886;

"the Rome Convention" means the International Convention for the Protection of Performers, Producers of Phonograms and Broadcasting Organisations done at Rome on 26 October 1961;

"the WPPT" means the World Intellectual Property Organisation Performances and Phonograms Treaty adopted in Geneva on 20 December 1996.

(10) A statutory instrument containing an Order in Council under this section is subject to annulment in pursuance of a resolution of either House of Parliament."

(5) In section 206 of that Act (rights in performances: qualifying countries, etc.), in subsection (1), in the definition of "qualifying country"—

(a) for paragraph (b) substitute—

"(b) another EEA state,",

(b) after that paragraph (but before the following "or") insert—

"(ba) the Channel Islands, the Isle of Man or Gibraltar,", and

(c) after paragraph (ba) (but before the following "or") insert—

"(bb) a country which is a party to the Rome Convention,".

(6) In that section, after subsection (3) insert—

"(4) Her Majesty may by Order in Council—

(a) make provision for the application of this Part to a country by virtue of paragraph (bb) or (c) of the definition of "qualifying country" in subsection (1) to be subject to specified restrictions;

(b) amend the definition of "qualifying country" in subsection (1) so as to add a country which is not a party to the Rome Convention;

(c) make provision for the application of this Part to a country added under paragraph (b) to be subject to specified restrictions.

(5) A statutory instrument containing an Order in Council under this section is subject to annulment in pursuance of a resolution of either House of Parliament."

(7) In that section, after subsection (5) insert—

"(6) In this section, "the Rome Convention" means the International Convention for the Protection of Performers, Producers of Phonograms and Broadcasting Organisations done at Rome on 26 October 1961."

(8) In section 208(5) of that Act (which, so far as it gives power to designate any of the Channel Islands or the Isle of Man, is superseded by the new section 206(1)(ba)) omit "any of the Channel Islands, the Isle of Man or".

(9) After section 212 of that Act insert—

"Supplementary

212A Power to amend in consequence of changes to international law

(1) The Secretary of State may by order amend this Part in consequence of changes to international law in the area of performance rights.

(2) An order under this section must be made by statutory instrument; and no order may be made unless a draft of it has been laid before and approved by a resolution of each House of Parliament."

PART 4

GENERAL

23 Power to make consequential or transitional provision etc.

(1) The Secretary of State may by order made by statutory instrument—

(a) make provision in consequence of a provision of this Act;

(b) make transitional, transitory or saving provision in connection with the commencement of a provision of this Act or of provision made under paragraph (a).

(2) An order under this section may amend, repeal, revoke or otherwise modify an enactment.

(3) The power conferred by this section is not restricted by any other provision of this Act.

(4) In this section, "enactment" includes—

(a) an enactment contained in subordinate legislation (within the meaning of the Interpretation Act 1978), and

(b) an enactment contained in, or in an instrument made under, an Act of the Scottish Parliament, an Act or Measure of the National Assembly for Wales or Northern Ireland legislation,

and references to an enactment include a reference to an enactment passed or made after the passing of this Act.

(5) A statutory instrument which contains an order under this section containing (whether alone or with other provision) provision that amends or repeals a provision of an Act of Parliament may not be made unless a draft of the instrument has been laid before, and approved by a resolution of, each House of Parliament.

(6) Subject to that, a statutory instrument which contains an order under this section containing (whether alone or with other provision) provision under subsection (1)(a) is subject to annulment in pursuance of a resolution of either House of Parliament.

24 Commencement, extent and short title

(1) The preceding provisions of this Act come into force on such day as the Secretary of State may by order made by statutory instrument appoint.

(2) An order under this section may appoint different days for different purposes.

(3) An amendment or repeal made by this Act has the same extent as the enactment being amended or repealed.

(4) Section 21 extends to England and Wales, Scotland and Northern Ireland.

(5) Section 23 extends to England and Wales, Scotland, Northern Ireland and the Isle of Man.

(6) This Act may be cited as the Intellectual Property Act 2014.

SCHEDULE

Section 19

MINOR AMENDMENTS TO THE PATENTS ACT 1977

Patent applications in or for WTO members

1 (1) In section 5 of the Patents Act 1977 (priority date), in subsection (5), after paragraph (a) insert—

"(aa) an application in or for a country (other than the United Kingdom) which is a member of the World Trade Organisation for protection in respect of an invention which, in accordance with the law of that country or a treaty or international obligation to which it is a party, is equivalent to an application for a patent under this Act;".

(2) In that subsection, for "such an application" substitute "an application for a patent under this Act".

(3) In that section, omit subsection (6).

Assertion of third party rights where application terminated

2 In section 20B of that Act (effect of reinstatement of patent application), after subsection (4) insert—

"(4A) The right conferred by subsection (4) does not become exercisable until the end of the period during which a request may be made under this Act, or under the rules, for an extension of the period referred to in section 20A(1)."

Adjustment of certain time periods to anniversary date model

3 (1) In each of the following provisions of that Act, for "the end of the period of two years beginning with" substitute "the second anniversary of"—

(a) section 37(5) and (9) (determination of right to patent after grant), and

(b) section 72(2)(b) (application to revoke patent).

(2) In section 74(4)(b) of that Act (proceedings where validity of patent may be in issue), for "before the end of the period of two years beginning with" substitute "on or before the second anniversary of".

References to "counsel"

4 (1) In section 52(4) of that Act (appeals), for "such other counsel" substitute "such other person who has a right of audience".

(2) In section 58(2) of that Act (disputes as to Crown use), for "counsel for the other party" substitute "the other party's legal representative".

Correction of typographical error

5 In section 60(7) of that Act (meaning of infringement: interpretation), in the definition of "Directive 2001/82/EC", for "Directive 2004/28" substitute "Directive 2004/28/EC".

European patent (UK): payment of renewal fee following restoration

6 In section 77 of that Act (European patents (UK)), after subsection (5) insert—

"(5A) Where, under the European Patent Convention, a European patent (UK) is revoked and subsequently restored (including where it is revoked by the Board of Appeal and subsequently restored by the Enlarged Board of Appeal), any fee that would have been imposed in relation to the patent after the revocation but before the restoration is payable within the prescribed period following the restoration."

Adapted and published by GRANGIS under the OGL Licence 3.0.

www.nationalarchives.gov.uk/doc/open-government-licence/version/3/

GRANGIS - UK PUBLISHING 2022.

www.ingramcontent.com/pod-product-compliance
Lightning Source LLC
LaVergne TN
LVHW060214210926
848481LV00008B/2741
9798885590556